AN
HONEST
DAY'S
ODE

NATHAN BROWN

MEZCALITA
PRESS

MEZCALITA PRESS, LLC
Norman, Oklahoma

MEZCALITA PRESS, LLC
Norman, Oklahoma

AN
HONEST
DAY'S
ODE

NATHAN BROWN

MEZCALITA
PRESS

TABLE OF CONTENTS

ACKNOWLEDGEMENTS

This is the second book in a trilogy I promised my daughter I'd have out before the end of 2017. Because of current cultural issues, this has been a dark and sad year for her. One that is testing her faith and trust in things. If it sounds like I'm being vague, I am. A father's love is as careful as it is hopeless and bottomless. So, Sierra, here is a book of odes for you to see and know what I still love about this world.

Thanks to the *Red Dirt Forum – Fall 2017* for first publishing the poems "Young Soldier" and "Fort."

Thanks to Jen Rickard Blair for such beautiful, consistent, and prompt design work.

Thanks, always, to my wife Ashley—the best partner and poetry editor you will find.

And, forever, thanks to my parents… who first taught me to read.

The moral
of my ode is this:
beauty is twice
beauty
and what is good is doubly
good
when it is a matter of two socks
made of wool
in winter.

~ Pablo Neruda
"Ode to My Socks"

AN HONEST DAY'S ODE

ODE TO THE ODE

You gave us a way to express
our big feelings about the little
things in life, one thing at a time.

A way to remember those things
we too often forget. Like the ode.

And, yes, you have been abused—
by the poets-come-lately who have
never read your finest examples, or
the college undergrad who refused
to even look up your definition.

Yet, you remain among us—
as those little and finer things
in life find a way of doing—

like a cute mouse that lives
in the wall and sneaks out
to clean up the crumbs
of our careless days
in the dark of night.

FRECKLES

It's the contrast they offer
to the perfection of a thing
like skin.
        A baby's face
may be beautiful, but
it lacks character still.

Few things outshine
the glory of the sun's
mad, passionate abandon
when dancing on a woman's
soft and shirtless shoulders.

And, the more experience
they have with each other,
all the more captivating is
the sultry and salty tango.
We can't help but admire
a routine well-rehearsed.

Of course, it's also true
that those darker shades
forebode certain dangers

of melanin gone wild—
the sun's deep burning
is both life and death.

But there is no blossom
that bursts onto the stage
of earth's extravagant opera
without that all-necessary
blast of solar radiation.

So, let us celebrate
the exquisiteness
of tonal variations,
and carry our marks
with pride and grace.

A SMILE

Whether you wear one
can modify the bearing
of a fellow traveler's day.

And, each one we meet
reminds us we were not
always the tired sourpuss
we've let ourselves become.

A well-aimed one can disarm
a malcontent—possibly even
a terrorist on his way to work.

And, whether a glum president
learns to wear one that looks real
may determine the continuation—
or the end—of the human species.

Either way, there's nothing wrong
with keeping one in your pocket.
And it will never hurt
to pull it out.

HONEYSUCKLE

So little return
on the meticulous
investment we put in,

that not-quite-a-drop
of not-quite-a-honey

pulled back through
the blossom's velvet
not-quite-a-trumpet,

by way of the stigma
attached to its style,

and yet a thousand
childhoods can be
relived in that tiny
bomb of nectar.

Young Soldier

You left home so full
of fear, and yet, a vague
sense of invincibility.

But now, years later,
what you saw there—
what you came to know
but not understand—

possesses you in a way
they could not have
prepared you for.

And though they pay
for your education,
you're not learning
what you need
to become
whole again.

But we are here.

And we appreciate
what you did for us...
what you've endured
that you can't, yet,
talk to us about.

And when you wake
at 3:00 am confused
about the enemy...

we are on your side.

We want to help with
this. The tougher war.

The one they may not
have warned you about.

The one you did not
see coming.

MUG WARMER

You keep alive
my favorite part
of every morning—

the part that keeps me
getting up and going—
the reading, the writing.

The first sip of coffee,
that reason for rising,
and each sip thereafter
that you keep warming.

And though scientists,
and the Surgeon General,
at times offer some warning,

it is you, and the coffee you keep,
that become the words on the page,
these words I am always forming.

FORT

It's one of the few spaces
we'll ever get to ourselves
that won't require rent
or a big mortgage—
    no water, gas,
     or electric bill.

And we don't care
that there's no TV,
because being hidden
from the rest of the world
is all the thrill we ever need.

The secrets told to no one—
thoughts we think nowhere else—
the love affairs we have with those
who will never know about it—

yes, all the furtive things we do,
and all those words unspoken,
that become all of those ways
we will survive growing up.

GUITAR

If not all objects are inanimate,
then this one, four feet away
and facing me, has surely
lived a long and worthy life.

For every scar and each dent,
it just began to sing louder.

And all the years it carried
my pain, only served us up
these years of deeper joys.

Wood and steel, a friend?

A valid question, maybe
for the skeptic, or stoic.

But not for the player.

TOP

It gets all the attention—
always up there, looking down
from the highest point of everything.

It feels like some way out, maybe,
of the lower parts of our lives—
like a new and better beginning.

Like the first poem in a book,
the one that encourages us,
hopefully, to read on.

Bottom

It has to be there—
some place for our feet
to hit, after that long drop.

Otherwise we just keep going
down and out into the other
stars. The ones we never see.

And though the landing may
hurt a bit, we need to get to it.
And sooner's better than later.

FRONT

It's the part of a thing we put most
of the design work into before
the product hits the shelf.

It's what turns a shopper
into a buyer. Or the door
that guests come through.

The part of the book we go
back to. And, usually, the first
thing at the scene of the accident.

BACK

This is where we put, you know,
the ingredients, the side-effects,
and all of the other fine print.

This is where the Baptists sit,
to better judge those in front.
Where we got spanked as a kid.

It's the hardest part of goodbye,
the thing we're most sorry to see
when someone slowly walks away.

BEGINNING

At the beginning, our feet
don't hurt yet, and we have
plenty of good provisions still.

The hero has not been tested.
And, God has only just recently
created the heavens and the earth.

We are bursting with a naïve hope.
And though we'll lose the naiveté,
we will try to hold on to the hope.

MIDDLE

The middle is where the plot
begins to slow and bog down,
until a huge mistake is made.

Then, the big guns come out.
The children don't understand.
And there may be a police chase.

This is when we decide to never
be normal again—to eat better—
begin lifting weights to loud music.

END

The end is when we realize
it's too late for some things,
but maybe not for the others.

The bridges are all ash heaps.
The villages, smoldering ruins
off in the distances behind us.

But, if the one we love is still
beside us, we'll make it—as we
wipe mud off each other's cheeks.

ACCIDENTAL DEATH INSURANCE

Because that possibility
is always out there…

I think about it every
time I get in the car—
or especially on a plane.

Besides, an intentional
or premeditated death
is out of the question.

I've got too many books
in the cue. And, my wife
needs me to go to the store
and get rid of the scorpions
that sneak inside our house.

And even more besides, life
is just so darn good, now,
and it took a long time,
fifty some odd years,

to get it that way.

But still, I know those
chicken bones and stray
bullets are out there…

everywhere.

So, I do appreciate
Farmers Insurance
thinking of me here
on my 52nd birthday.

But, I think I'll pass.

WIND

God-breath.
A bit of a breeze
stirring up conversation
in the community of leaves.

A gentle reminder of air
and our ultimate need
for it—inside and out.

Air that, when it becomes
unstable, tilts the shear
to form an upright vortex
in an Oklahoma thunderstorm,

and then all wind breaks loose
in that early-summer shredder
of the greening Great Plains.

But, even when it comes in
too hard, and too strong,
we need what it carries away
as much as we do what it brings.

It's the original nomad—
the uncle who never stays
whenever he comes to visit.

We wave hello when we face it
in the summer's morning sun.

We wave goodbye when we
turn away from it in the cold
of a moonless winter's night.

And… just like the rain…

we do not live without it.

RAIN

Just the tapping of it
on a metal roof is one
of my favorite grooves.

Maybe the cymbal crash
of thunder mixed with it.

Giving the cattle and corn
a much-needed sip of what
gives all of us the chance
to go on with ourselves.

We'd have no ice cream
or soft tortillas without it.

We forget that sometimes,
the things that come from
all the plants and animals
that sing the water song.

Yes, if the skies didn't fall,
there'd be no banana pudding

after dinner for you, young man.

And yet, when it shows up
in relentless downpours,
we soon find ourselves
rolling up the area rugs,

running for high ground,
suddenly up Noah's creek
without any kind of paddle.

The rivers and streams commit
their long-awaited coup d'état
against human encroachment
and our claims on property.

But even as we're mopping
the floors and carrying out
the couch and bed to dry
in the next day's sun,

we know…

down inside
the parts of us
that first walked
the plains of earth...

that the rain must come.

So... let it come.

SNAIL

What joy to see above me
the little guy who'd made it

up to the high part of the eave,
fifteen feet from the ground—

yet as still as the sun shining
over an August afternoon,

reminding me that great
distances can be covered

imperceptibly, that a lifetime
of millimeters and good effort

could, someday, result in
a much better view.

THERAPY

Who doesn't love a safe place
to speak one's mind—to say
the things we would not say
in other spaces, even ones
that seem relatively safe?

Where we go for another
person to finally listen in
on the long conversation
we have been carrying on
with ourselves since birth.

Where we fear to find out
the things about ourselves
we did not want to know,

but someone close to us
felt that it was high-time
we found out anyway.

And more power to us,

and to them as well,

for, high-time
is high-time.

And so…

I look forward
to the next session.

TACO TRUCK

For being consistent
with fresh ingredients…

yet mysterious and elusive
when it comes to location.

For taking the time necessary
to cook the tempura shrimp
while I stand there waiting

(so that it is crackling-hot)
then assembling, by hand,
all of that greasy goodness

slathered in coleslaw, with
the best cilantro lime aioli
in town, and all pour moi.

And for letting me order
only one, without those
unnecessary side dishes.

For giving me an umbrella

for shade at the picnic table
by the massive live oak tree.

And for forcing me to use
an untended Port-a-Potty
in the 95-degree heat—

reminding me to always
be grateful for the indoor
plumbing in our house.

THE WORST OF IT

The darkest hours…
    the longest nights…
life's personal cataclysms,

when things go from dark
to blackest black in a flash
of hot jagged lightning—

things we'd thought only
happened to other people
or other people's children,

she is alive,
        but…
                or, he is not.

The moments we decide
that it's time to learn how
to properly fold the flag,

when we come to grips with
how much we hate the ER—
or the lobby of an oncologist.

Those times that force us
to realize what it all is
and isn't worth, when

we pour more wine,
and it doesn't matter,
and no one blames us,

when we sell most of it,
throw or give the rest away,
and move into a smaller place,

when we have to think…
        long and hard…
before making that call,

when we finally quit the job,
slam the boss's big oak door,
and just walk right out of there,

when we look 'em in the eye,
without blinking, and say
that it's over… done.

The day we decide to die—
which is okay, nothing wrong
with it. Or, we determine that

there will come a new day…
we can do this thing… and
something will come of it.

GIN & TONIC

For being so hard to screw up,
when sitting at a bar in a town
in a part of the country where
you know they won't be able
to make a good margarita
to save anybody's life.

For delivering a similar joy
on nights when the marriage
of your lips to a lowball glass
is the only chance for love.

So… a toast!

To the hard truths
    of simplicity…

        and, to the need
        for artlessness when
        the occasion calls for it.

STORYTELLER

~ for U.P. and G.K.

You make life better…

    better than it was,
    better than it is,
    and likely better
    than it'll ever be.

You turn a deaf ear
to facts when it leads
to some higher truth—
and a blind eye to what
"actually happened,"
when what we don't
know will make us
the better for it.

And, you carry
the weight of
the white lie
for our sakes.

PETIT FOUR

For being a hint,
a survivable sample,

of that culinary decadence
that would otherwise send us
to an early and extra-large grave.

Of course, we always eat more
than one, because there are so
many varieties and flavors—

and because we just happen
to be passing by the table…
again… for the fourth time.

And for meaning *small oven*
in French. As if anyone has
an oven that small. I mean,
could you be… any cuter?

SPILLED MILK

You can be beautiful,
especially on a dark surface,
puddled up, or spread out—
an accident of chiaroscuro.

Like the unexpected child…

> *We're alright. It has happened
> now. We can make this work.*

And yet, I have to admit
I *have* cried over you—
even though there is
no use in doing so.

Some days are just
harder than others.

And that milk, jeez,
is now dripping from
the counter to the floor.

And, for some reason,

that is the last straw.

But, even as we mop,
we know that Cheerios,
cupcakes, and hot chocolate
are nothing without what it is
that you bring to the table,

when properly contained
in a carton or bottle.

JALAPEÑO

O sharp, curved fruit,
shaped like a little dagger,

how you remind us that even
the softest foods, like avocados
or refried beans, should not
go down without a fight,

that sometimes flavor
comes with a sting—

that a green and growing
thing can still burn our eyes
like the waters of the Dead Sea.

Even on the morning after,
you come with a price.

SANITY

You seem so malleable…
an entirely different thing
in each different mind,

defined in roughly 7.5
billion different ways.

What power for a mere
six-letter word to have.

You are elusive and aloof,
and you're not a very good
communicator, by the way.

And yet… I do love it
when you pop in
for a visit.

DICTIONARY

For those many of us
who aren't know-it-alls,
you hold the answers.

And the way you stick,
so strictly, to the alphabet,
makes it substantially easier
to find what we're looking for.

How else would I have discovered,
on the first page, that an "abbess" is
the head of a community of nuns?

Or, way back at the very end,
that a "zygote" is a cell
formed by the union
of two gametes?

And, there are legions
of linguistic wonders between
those two, my friend, that
I still don't know about.

It's true, I've not read you
cover to cover, I'll admit.

But, there are many books
that I've not done the same,

quickly donating them to
the Salvation Army, or
a library fundraiser.

You… I keep.

TEXTING

You, the only way
my daughter lets me
know that she is alive,

as well as the only way
she will allow me to ask.

You, my wife's favorite
means to hustle me for
a glass of Topo Chico
and half a warm bagel

when she's still in bed
and knows that I am
writing in the library
but feels pretty sure
that I'll be a sweetie
and bring it anyway.

You're not as good as
other more direct forms
of human communication,

but, even my dear mother,
in her mid-eighties, learned
to speak your stunted lingo
and seems to really enjoy
all your cute little emojis.

So, what am I to do…
except try to get better
at typing with my thumbs?

GLOBE

The joy in spinning it
as a child, on its stand
in the library. The silent
whirling in a silent space.

The growing sense that we
could fly right off this thing
any minute of a 24-hour day.

Our first understanding that
there are just as many stars
below us, as above.

And then the other joy
in stopping it with a finger
to read the name of a country
that we did not know… yet…
was a very tough place to live.

That there were the countries
in the world that did not have

libraries, let alone globes atop
stands for the children there
to spin and stop with a finger.

A good thing to remember...
as a grown man now standing
in my own library, spinning
the one that my parents
handed down to me.

PURITY

is an acquired taste.

Not a thing we are
necessarily used to—

the absolute and undiluted
version of a thing, like coffee
or sex—the life experiences that
usually begin with sugar or cream
or soft porn… or, say, the prom.

For some weird reason, we speak
of Native Americans and chocolate
in terms of percentages or fractions.

My Cherokee-ness hovers around
1/16 to 1/32 because I get it from
both sides of my family tree and
therefore, it is confusing—and
because a few of my forefathers
refused to sign the government rolls.

The Divine Chocolate Bar I bought
states it is 70% Dark Chocolate
and claims to be Fair Trade,
NON GMO Verified,
and Halal Certified—

which is a whole other
discussion on untaintedness
altogether that I'll not go into.

But, more and more, I love
to get down to the essence
of the better things in life.

The reason I love poetry.

HOUSE PLANT

You are among those
we invite to come inside
and sit with us by a window.

Not that it's something
you would want to do.

But we love having you
here beside us. And you
add oxygen to the rooms
where we simply suck it up.

That makes you better than us,
as far as the earth is concerned.

And that reconnection to what
matters, is something that we
need and thank you for.

RUSH HOUR

We need the stuff in life
that reminds us there is

not   one   thing
we can do about it.

This is where we are
stuck. And that is now
what time we are not
going to get there.

So, relax a bit—
dial up a favorite
meditation podcast
and enjoy the ride.

Even this one.

PAPERBACKS

For the way you bend
into pockets and backpacks,
drawers and glove compartments,

a good story any and everywhere
we can tuck it, or cram it into,
always ready and there for us.

For the way that your battery
never dies, o travel companion
with no USB wires or adaptors,

and that, when the coffee spills,
we do not have to buy the new
slick 399-dollar version of you.

We just wipe you off and shake
you out, and then let you dry
while we read Chapter 4.

SKIN

For all that you contain,

for as long as you contain it,
sometimes a hundred years,

you are shockingly easy
to slice and open up—

    everything that matters
    quickly draining away.

And yet, the ability to heal,
to regrow and cover up…

stretch, wrinkle, and sag,
without giving it all up…

my God, what a thing
we forget you are.

POPCORN

The firework that froze
mid-explosion, banging
on the lid of the cooker
in its dreams of flight.

The speck of moisture
in the belly that turned
into steam, dying for
some way to get out,

and boom, the kernel
became a white cloud
crossing over the sun
of distant childhoods.

With way too much
salt and fake butter,
it too saw the movies
in those dark theaters.

And Wednesday nights
were "popcorn night,"

Dad's humpday treat,
marking every week.

And so, it will forever
be the taste of a time
before life and love,
software and taxes,

got so complicated.

MATCH

When we need
just enough fire
to get another one
started—a grain of red
phosphorus turning white,

    the heat that then ignites
    the potassium chlorate,

and whoosh, the volatile
hot-head-on-a-stick
bursts into flame.

And yet, we know
not to take its lesser size
for granted, like a split atom,

because it has brought down
homes, entire cities, even vast
regions of pristine forestland.

But there are also the times,

and certain situations, when
we may very well die without
this tiny hero's one superpower.

So we, the everyday citizens
of Gotham, would like
to thank you for all
you've done for us.

BUKOWSKI

For making it okay
to be myself—
by being so
much worse.

For showing me
that PhDs mostly
just know a lot more
about one or two things
and often sacrifice by
knowing a lot less
about the stuff
that makes
life bearable.

For so many books
that read like ice cream.
I know they're bad for me.
But, God… I love 'em.

For lines like "angels
are flying low tonight
with burning wings,"

and "love breaks my
bones and I
laugh."

You were
the unforgivable
chauvinistic prophet
stoned by the city gates
for the rest of us who
are all just as un-
redeemable.

lines taken from
The People Look Like Flowers at Last

Spam®

O mystery meat—
mostly pork shoulder
with nitrates n' nitrites.

O 48 grams of total fat,
skillet-fried with apples,
onion and pineapple bits.

And I do not know why,
but here, on a Tuesday,
listening to KC & the

Sunshine Band sing
"Afternoon Delight,"
I now vaguely recall

cutting you into cubes
and stuffing you into
a hollowed pineapple

to bake in the coals
of a dying campfire
in my mopey youth.

Was it Cub Scouts,
or church camp, or
some other torture?

The things we called
food back in the 1970s,
confound the imagination,

back when the petroleum
and the food industries
were indistinguishable.

SPIDER HOUSE

O coffee shop
that doesn't open
until 11:00 am—so
you can serve tequila
with lunch—which is
breakfast for alcoholics,

where I do actually order
coffee, and not the tequila.

For all your dark corners,
garage-sale chairs—and
the ridiculous number
of multi-colored
twinkle lights.

Flies banging on
paint-stained windows
nailed shut, and UT kids
studying right next to UT
kids who are day-drinking,
when they should be studying.

For the odd background music,
the chipped statues of saints,
and tattered oil paintings
of dead rich people
with no names
on plaques...

and no one
to care.

80s Music

O decade, My decade,
of the DX7 synthesizer
and drum machines…

all hooked up together
with MIDI cables so that
they could talk each other
into creating the scapes
behind all my whining
about girls and God.

That decade when
I only *thought* I had
stuff to worry about.

Problems I worked out
with lockstep sequences
of quarter, eighth, and—
at times—sixteenth notes.

The basic math of a white
seventeen-year-old male
living in the Great Plains.

I did what I could.

And I now thank God
for God and the girls—
the two most inspirational
thorns in my pubescent side.

ALONE TIME

For an hour,
maybe a few days,
you come, here and
there, to remind me

just how much I love
the few people I love,
and yet, how much
I love to be alone.

And, how much
I will always ache
for a bit of the other
whenever I have the one.

And, how it will forever
be a little hard… and
a little wonderful…
at the same time.

BLUE

To be both the color
of the vaulted sky, and

the saddest kind of song
where love ain't never
gonna treat you right.

To be one of the colors
of a bruise, and yet also
the blazing, beautiful
eyes of my daughter.

To be one of three
roots of all colors,

a primary pigment
on the wet palette
of Van Gogh...

the canvas
of Monet.

RED

They say you're the color
of my heart. But I would say,
it's more complicated than that.

I imagine many shades and hues,
smashed cherries on a sidewalk,
a hard pickled beet with a limp.

And yet, you're also the color
of what I feel for my Ashley
when she touches my chest.

While, all at the same time,
you represent anger, every
thing in life that burns us.

Mercury and Mars, gods
and planets, and other
related problems.

YELLOW

The sun would be the go-to
image for you—though it is
too painful to look up into
to verify if that's the case.
Daisies and bananas, taxis
and school buses, predictable.

So, to know that you are also
connected to jealousy and fear,
even deception and depression,
keeps us just this side of those
more sappy-go-lucky thoughts,
and the onslaught of too many
thinkally thoughts, since you are
also the color of creative hyper-
activity and Winnie-the-Pooh,
leaving us tapping foreheads
and wondering all day long
how to get that honey
out of the bottom
of the jar.

RUM & COKE

Because cocktails and day-drinking
should have dessert on the menu.

Because, if I'm going to break
my vegetarian vows for a day,
I'll need something to go with
the ribs at Miller's Smokehouse
down in Belton, Texas. Oh yeah.

Come on… I am not going to not
celebrate my uncle's 90th birthday.
He has earned my collusion, no?

Because… like the gin & tonic,
there's no way to screw it up—

just add Coke, or, more likely,
more rum, until it tastes right.

And because, if I'm gonna read
Bukowski going off on the time
he had to give up the smokes
and the bottle for six months,

because of the tuberculosis
there towards the end
of his crazy, boozy,
star-crossed life…

I'm gonna need
a drink.

SAUSAGE BISCUIT

Because breakfast should have
its sandwiches too… O petite
hamburger-o'-the-morning,
mornings now long past.

You usually signified
I'd been left to my own
and ill-advised devices, or

that we were on the road
to Colorado for a vacation
and had stopped somewhere
at a drive-thru along I-40 West.

Whether Jimmy Dean snack-size,
at Hardees, or a McDonald's,
I loved, and I've paid for,
that greeezy goodness.

SUMMER SOLSTICE

Hump day for the whole year.

Not the hottest, but certainly
the beginning of the sun's
headline on how much
we will suffer in August.

And even if our dripping
popsicles and swimsuits
grant us the delusion
of cooling off a bit,
we know the planet
is cranking the dial on
its displeasure over our
haymaking and saturnalia.

And so, if it means only
that I get to go outside
a little earlier, I'll take
an extra minute or so
of night, each day.

WINDOW

What a dank place
the house would be
without you there
dotting the walls.

And where else
would a poet stare
when inspiration wains?

In summer, you're the way
we live at peace with the sun,
when it would kill by degrees
if we dared to go outdoors.

In winter, you're the way
to enjoy a snowstorm
and a smart book
at the same time.

Transparent yet solid,
like we wish government
could somehow someday be,

and yet still with a clear set
of rules and conditions
on the relationship—
      as it should be.

And you've just shown me
the rose bush is in bloom,

and that the two boy-cats
are doing just fine, rolling
around in dirt and grass.

So, I wrote this poem
to tell you how much
I appreciate the updates.

SCONE

For being a cookie
disguised as bread…

and so, making us feel
the slightest bit superior

and somewhat in control
of our depraved appetites

when we sit in coffee shops
next to some self-conscious

gourmand who is crouched
over a most immoderate slice

of pineapple upside-down cake.

iTunes

I hate to admit it,
but, I do love you...

the way you allow me
to relive life, my youth,
by decades and seasons.

You can play the very song
that was on the radio when
I held hands with Irene—
a blond Norwegian twin,
no joke—in the back seat
of our gymnastics coach's
AMC Pacer in 7th grade,
Rod Stewart croaking out
"Do Ya Think I'm Sexy."
O be still, my heart.

And, Irene prefers
women these days.
But... that night?

That heady night,
we were "a thing."

Or, say, Duran Duran's
"Hungry Like the Wolf"
back as an awkward junior
driving my grandmother's
ancient Mercury Comet
while my friend, Roland,
stuffed his foot-wide afro
into the glove box looking
for some squirrel running
in a little round cage—
the thing he just knew
was powering the engine.

We called it the Red Bomb,
because my first car had been
a hand-me-down station wagon
known as The Great White Tank.
Or, just The Tank, for short.

Ah, the '70s and '80s…
two of my favorites…

but you have no '90s
in the library, let alone
on some playlist—
a dark decade where
pop music went to die.

But, at Christmas time?
There are no words to say
how much you mean to me
during those cool-down days
between Thanksgiving's turkey
and the Baby Jesus's Big Night.

And, let me count the ways
you've saved my marriage,
when it comes to limited
storage space and all.

FIRST CAR

One of the great
embarrassments
early lives require.

A rite of our passage
into the much greater
embarrassments ahead,

a hard lesson in how to take
what we are handed, slide on
a pair o' dark shades, and drive
that old sucker like we mean it.

One of the most important
skills we will ever learn
for succeeding…
or surviving.

YELLOW STRIPES

Because some rules are not
meant to be broken. You—
that ominous divide between
evolved primates with car keys
traveling at questionable speeds
in two very different directions.

You, the perfectly broken line
down the middle, telling us,
like the buzzy warning sign
of a hornet's banded back,

that there might be a price
if we mess with territories.
Yet you lead and guide us
to the most beautiful spaces,

the wide-open backroad places
that remind us how the earth
is, still, not something
to give up on.

ROTATION

The tire around the axel,
taking us out to the oceans
or mountains of our day-
dreams and vacations—

or away from whatever
it is that must be left.

*

The dizzying contrapuntal
spinning of the ball rolling
against the roulette wheel,
like the Cheshire Cat's eyes,

messing with our balance
because a small fortune
is riding on that thing.

*

The necessary rule, or law,
that keeps the open-mic poet,
or the hidden-pocket politician,
from metastasizing in the body.

*

The earth around its shifting axis,
saving us from having to choose
between living in constant light,
or night's relentless darkness.

SILENCE

You are as rare these days
as a Northern Hairy-Nosed
Wombat in Queensland.
Critically endangered,

and somewhere deep
in the jungles of South
America, that we haven't
burned down yet, hidden
like an undiscovered plant
that could cure everything.

You once ranged the entire
planet—back in the epochs
before homo sapiens created
batteries and lawn equipment.

And as with all things unfamiliar,
we fear you now. You've become
like the great white shark lurking
in the doldrums of our downtime
and days off from numbing jobs.

So, we've installed networks
of television, created force fields
powered by iTunes and headphones,

and burn every ounce of combustion
we can muster… to keep you at bay.

But please don't give up on us.
We may find our way home.

INDEX FINGER

We do not realize
the all of everything
you do, until you are cut
deep, and in total disrepair.

When the simple act of a fork
through French toast, or this pen
applying words to a page, pump
drops of hot blood to mingle
with the syrup and the ink.

We forget that you have
your own pulsing heart
that breaks and flutters,
palpitates and murmurs,
just like our bigger ones.

So… please find your way
to healing as soon as you can.

I've become bored, and boring
to my sweet dog who wants
to go for a longer walk.

My guitar is fretting
over on its stand
in the corner.

And, my wife
has a few things
she'd like for me
to get done 'round
the house sooner
rather than
later.

CLOUDY DAYS

You're one of my favorite ways
to venture out into the world.

You give the troposphere
a little shady ambiance—

draperies… furniture…
a lamp here and there.

Sunny days are relentless
in their lack of variation.

And the sun never allows
us to observe its moving.

But, you can't be every day.
'Cuz I'd get tired of that too.

WEATHER FORECASTER

Your wide-eyed excitement
over what will most likely be

the grave misfortune of those
caught dead-center in the path,

makes it hard to appreciate you.
But we do—especially for the

extra time you give us to run
for the cellar or to board up

all the windows and doors.
You, in your bright dresses

and bold ties—reminding us
that even the sunniest of days

have their ways of doing us in.

ODE TO AN ELEGY

To figure out how to say
what it is that we likely
should have said
before now.

Or, in some cases,
what we could not say
before now, because we
would not have meant it,

as we do not mean it now,
but here we are all gathered,
and something must be said.

Or, to figure out what it is
that we should be saying
all along and well before
it is too late to say it—

to lament, praise, then
console those we love
before we lose them,

instead of the others
who once knew them.

To kiss their wet cheeks,
hug their still-warm necks.

To touch their hands
and hearts, instead
of the coffin's lid.

PLEDGE OF ALLEGIANCE

~ for the 4th of July

Well… Happy 241st Birthday
to the United States of America,

by which we sit in folding chairs
next to huge ice chests and stuff
our faces and bellies with beer,
barbecue, oh and that pinkish,
part JELL-O® salad that only
grandma knows how to make,

as we pledge some allegiance
to the flags on all our t-shirts
that are stained with hot sauce
and grease, and made in China.

I would wish to have been born
in no other Nation under God,
and the good care of my parents
in my Norman of Oklahoma—

a state where faith and patriotism
are indivisible, and yet I somehow
managed to find a good amount
of liberty and justice for myself,
because I'm mostly Cherokee,
but, since I seldom get a tan
in the scorch of summer sun,
I, basically, appear to be white.

And so, I state, hard and clear:
This is my home, this is my land.
This is my nation and my country.
And my love for birds, butterflies,
and the music of John Denver—
along with a belief in nonviolence,
basic human – and animal – rights,
and justice for all shades of skin—
does not… make me… any less
of a patriot… or a native son.

SHOVEL

I spend some quiet hours
with you among the oaks,
cactus, and the cedar thickets
of our extra lot where, sometimes,
I spend a few too many quiet hours
with you, according to a good wife.

But you're how I collect stones
and clear out paths, play hide-
and-seek with the joy of what
lies just underneath the surface:
dirt, grubs, and the suburban
sprawl of ants and spiders.

There is also, of course,
the simple act of digging
a hole down into the earth,
and how standing and staring
at it afterwards reminds me
that I worry way too much.

DIPLOMA

You remind me of days, years,
I both miss and would never…
not for any… thing… repeat.
Over two decades I gave to

a university that, in the end,
gave nothing back in the way
of a job, health insurance, or
hopes for retiring someday.

But you… you hang low
on the green wall, next to
my writing desk, and whistle
while I work each morning,

making sure I do not forget
that anyone who starts to act
a bit too mean, or snotty, may
refer to me as "Dr. Brown."

THAT TREE

Yes, there was one specific one.
In the schoolyard by Iowa Street.

I spent strange amounts of time
in a cradle-weave of big limbs
up near the very top. An elm.
Before my teens. Definitely
during. And probably after.

I'm 52 now, and I still go
check on it when I visit
my parents in Norman.

Because, it was there,
in that me-sized nest,
I dreamed of being older.

And any age would've done.
Any number higher than mine.
And see?   I've made it!

And, it was there I dreamed
of finding a golden-limbed girl

someday, who'd be sexy and true.
Bam. Check that one off the list too.

And, it was there I dreamed of
becoming a world-famous
music-scene sensation.

And, well, now,
I'm a poet.

Because...
                you can't have it all.

BASSOON

O stepchild of
the woodwinds,

the class's clown
whose edgy humor

wells up from a dark
corridor of the tragedy.

So low… you are forced
to bend your neck to keep

from hitting the stage floor.
That gruff older brother,

and the big deep voice,
of the Oboe Family—

usually hanging out with
the tubas and trombones,

and always on the other side
of the tracks from first violins.

You hang back in the realm
of hidden things—and yet,

if you ever left the orchestra,
we'd wonder what was wrong,

what happened to Handel and
his suite for the Royal Fireworks,

or Mozart's "Sinfonia Concertante
for Four Winds in E Flat Major."

TEQUILA

There are some problems
that help us in certain ways.

There are some nights when
nothing but a certain problem

will do for the day we've had.
And there are certain friends

we can get enough of—
so, it is time for them

to gather their things
and get back home.

But, there is a reason
certain bottles've been

on the shelf at the store
since the Neolithic period.

There are even more reasons,
many more, why those bottles

have become a certain amount
of trouble for certain people

through those 12,000 years.
And so, as we well know,

there are the certain times
when slow's the way to go.

MEDICINE

What you are
changes weekly,
according to recent
studies by authorities.

What saved us last year
is our impending demise
as of this evening's news.

And, do I have to say:
        vice versa?

Today, it's coffee.
Tomorrow it will be
that daily glass of wine
you, and the apostle Paul,
once promised us was a gift
from the good Lord himself.

What's a poet, or plumber,
to do, I'd ask—besides
drink a bit of both
every day.

Look…
if the choice is
between some mass-
produced petrochemical pills

or the long, time-honored process
of slow-baking the blue agave *piñas*,

followed by shredding and mashing
under the *tahona*, that stone wheel,

to squeeze out that precious juice
they then ferment to perfection,
as well as to my health…

you do not need
to ask again.

TOILET

To be honest with ourselves,
about things we seldom think
to remember we might ought to,

you stand out among
the advances that made
civilization what it is today.

Like refrigeration, fermentation,
lights and switches and the splitting
of atoms, you changed everything.

You—along with those small rolls
of special paper that some other
invented—eased one of life's

most messy and smelly and
undoubtedly unavoidable
business transactions.

But you also gave us a space
where reasonable people know
we'd prefer to be left alone.

Not to mention the quick
and convenient way to hide
pieces of smoking evidence.

And when you came indoors?
You made January and August
much more bearable to live with.

And when you clog, or you back up?
We're suddenly honest with ourselves
about how desperately we need you…

and we suddenly think to remember
that we might ought to take
better care of you.

THE PAINTER

The member of the arts family
who doesn't feel the need
to say much, before,
during, or after
her oily work.

The pigment
does the talking.

And what it goes on
about, is their business.

And the language has no words.
That's why her favorite title
will always be: "Untitled."

GARBAGEMAN

You are the savior-come-lately,
carrying the weight of our sins
and all that we could not eat,
because we were just stuffed,

on your shoulders, and in big
smelly trucks—off to massive
purgatorial mountains of waste,
that we might forget and forgive

ourselves for the billion plastic
wrappers and Styrofoam cups
that will blow in the hot breeze
of our grandchild's inheritance.

White Man

You are your favorite dream
that cannot come true—

because you never were
to begin with.

In the few degrees
of separation required

for humans to continue
walking up on hind legs,

somewhere in your past
some Spaniard slept with

an Egyptian maid who
gave birth to a son who

then slept with a Cherokee,
don't you know it, princess,

who gave birth to a daughter
who made love to the idea

of what you believe you are.
And, that idea accomplished

some nice things. Minneapolis
is beautiful in early summer.

But, you remain an idea.
Which remains an idea

you seem unable
to grasp.

MORNING SUN

First rays have set
the fence on fire...

wooden slats glowing
like an oven's grate...

and, once again it appears
Earth didn't die in the night.

The wrens have hymnals out,
singing their early mass. And I

take communion with the bread
my mother made... coffee black.

The body and blood of whatever
made the glory of all this possible.

SUMMER STORM

You don't solve
the bigger problem
of the season's rage…

but you help us believe
the days may come again
when the sun and sidewalk

don't treat our bare feet
like hamburger patties
on a charcoal grill,

the car-door handle
does not raise a blister
on the thumb after work,

and we won't sweat-stain
our favorite old t-shirts
on a midnight stroll.

HOLY BIBLE

You lie
on your side
about eight inches
from my head as I write
in this library each morning.

A tool I now use to refer back
to the psychosis and saving grace
of a good Southern upbringing.

And, when I work to justify
the righteous anger I have
been trying to recover from
for the last seventeen years,

you remind me of the Lord
God Almighty from whom
it was passed down to me.

The Creator of genetic
flaws and dispositions.

But you still tell a number
of our better stories. Novels
these days tend to bog down
in the mud and wet grass of
intentional obfuscation and
existential self-doubting,
if not self-loathing.

And, you taught me
that a good man doesn't
just walk on by someone
injured and lying in a ditch.

And that, when the restless
idiots out in the crowd reach
for their guns, it's a good time
to squat down and draw
a fish or something
in the sand.

INSTRUMENTAL MUSIC

If English, my mother
tongue, is a farm pond,
then you are a great ocean.

A language so understated,
so vast, it takes a lifetime
to gain a partial fluency.

I've come to appreciate
the art that has no use for
the dire limitations of words.

That's why shorter poems
have so much more
to say.

SCRABBLE

Good, clean, wooden fun
for sharp, witty linguaphiles
who like to revel in their smarts.

A game I do not enjoy—not
because I am not smart, but
because I toil with the letters
of the alphabet and their words
every day in, and every day out.

I labor to piece together symbols
I have drawn from the chaotic pile
at the center of a semantic universe

in the hope of forming units that will
add up to so much more than your
little subscript numbers placed,
insidiously, in the lower
right-hand corner
of your tiles.

TOAST

Were you first
an accident of fire?

Maybe someone left a loaf
too close to the dying coals?

And which came first… you?
Or the butter… or the jelly?

And, could your founders
have imagined that someday
we would invent an appliance
that does nothing but turn
a slice of bread into you?

Did you ever dream
you would one day
become an industry?
An icon of everyday life?

A burnt offering on the side
of every breakfast combo plate
in every diner across the land?

And that you would come
with a variety of choices:
white, whole wheat, rye,
or, lately, sprouted grain?

Or that the Brits would
require your presence
at morning tea?

Do you resent
the way we use you
to sop up every ounce
of the runny egg yolks?

And, do you have plans
to retire anytime soon?

SPANISH

French is the language
I've most wanted to learn,
like the books on our shelves
that we've most wanted to read
but never have, and likely never will,
but we keep them on shelves anyway
to impress the people that we most
want to know, but likely never will.

Such a complicated sadness.

But you—you are the language
I have most needed to learn.

The language that conquered,
some 500 years ago, the land
of my birth that is still home.

And, the language most likely
to conquer it again before long.

You… the tongue that Neruda used
to seduce a million pearl-skinned lovers.

You... the heart's beat
and the black-booted rage
pounding the hard-wood floor
inside the cloud of dust and pain
swirling at the center of flamenco's
torment and beautiful madness.

You... with no word for *hokey*,
completely unafraid to rhyme
your flamboyant passions
and shameless lust.

I will get to know you,
or I will die a lesser man
in my corner of this country.

WEDDING

One of our finer,
and more splendid,
occasions of suspended
disbelief, a play we stage
a thousand times a day
in a thousand different
villages, towns, and cities.

Some young couple crying
in the throes of their sweet
and wholly necessary naïveté
that causes the long-married
an actual pain in their sides.

Some older couple crying
in the throes of their deep
gratitude from the shock
of how awfully inglorious
their first attempt, or two,
was, in retrospect. And so,
now they are terribly happy
here at what appears to be,

fingers crossed, a much better
second, or third, swing at the ball.

And one old odd couple laughing,
who've been corralled here today
in the eyes, and by the insistence,
of their loved ones, for the fifth,
or even sixth, go 'round because
they love a good party… and…
their loved ones… frankly…
are sick n' tired of them
playing the field.

MY HEAD

It has its own little heart,
long-broken, up in there.

But it learned to love again,
out the other side of the last
twenty to thirty years or so.

There was a time, though—
summer of 2004, maybe 5—
when it packed up all its bags
and said that it was leaving me.

And it sounded like it meant it.

But, after giving some thought
(as it is far too inclined to do)
it decided to stay and maybe
try to work something out.

So, we've been in therapy
for years and really seem
to be in a new place now.

The good doctor has given us
some tools and ways to better
understand each other's quirks
and electro-chemical glitches.

But, I swear, if our friends
had any idea… any real
taste of the craziness
goin' on up in there,

they'd call the police.

WORLD PEACE

Now that you've become a tweet,
and've long been a bumper sticker,
we've tuned out your beggar's voice.

You're a thing we love to remember,
when the news is all terror and bombs,
but're too tired to unpack and dust off.

Quarantined now in the realm of wishes,
you have become a permanent concept,
that big-mouth going off at every party

that no one bothers to believe anymore.
The only hope left being that the young
and naïve will continue to be young

and naïve enough to continue
to have faith in things
like comebacks.

OUR SONS

When the rules change faster
than genetics can compensate for,
we need to understand the hot war
DNA's waging deep in their atoms.

All that nature and survival
trained them for, for tens
of thousands of years,
turns out not to be
what women wanted.

Now, the fire-breathing
dragon's on the endangered
list, the trash needs taking out,
and they are to remember to get
roses at the store on the way home.

So, be patient. Work with them.
Evolution takes centuries.

OUR DAUGHTERS

To ask forgiveness
for some 200,000 years
of getting it terribly wrong,
would be like moving the shores
of the Pacific inland, one grain
of washed-up sand at a time.

But, we owe them as much
reparation as we can muster,
dear God. And, by the way,
dear God… much of it is
your fault—or… at least
the fault of your officially
sanctioned, if not self-
proclaimed, spokesmen.

Is it their preciousness
and beauty that undoes
us males who objectify
or mistreat them? Until,

sometimes but not always,
we turn into our fathers?

And then the guilt over
what we did in our earlier
lust-empowered ignorance,
turns out to be more than
we could possibly bear?

So, we turn into raving
lunatics who punish them
for making us feel so bad?

Whatever it was, and is,
something went wrong
so far back there…
no one recalls.

OUR CHILDREN

We dole out inexcusable
excesses of what they never
wanted or ever required of us,
running up and down the aisles
of ToysRUs seeking absolution.

It took almost twenty-one years
of half-listening to my daughter
to figure out that what she had
most hoped for was—for me
to simply listen to her. Duh.

We give them cash or credit
and send them off to malls,
Taco Bells, and universities,

when what they need more
is to learn how to make it,
and then spend less of it.

Far too many of them
are diamonds falling

down through layers
of refuse in a trash heap
of wi-fi and reality television.

And so, we must decide, soon,
how dirty we're willing to get.

Not to mention how deep
we are willing to go.

FAITH

I commit acts of you every day,
by going back out into the world
again—in spite of all the evidence.

And yet, our relationship thrives
by keeping a certain distance.

Meaning, I had to let you go
if I was ever going to find
God, being elusive as she is.

At the same time, without you
I never would have married
my remarkably better
second wife.

So, when I say,
"Let you go," I hope
you won't think I intended
for you to leave altogether.

Because, I'm now learning
that to live without you

takes a lot of the luster
out of life's thick hide.

To say that I don't care
for the God of Leviticus,
Numbers, and Deuteronomy,

does not mean that I don't
like the one that appears
in the Gospel of John.

And so, if you're willing,
I want us to keep working
on our necessary negotiations.

HOPE

I lost you a few times…

but you kept sneaking up
behind and alongside me
as I made my way through
"that savage forest, dense
and difficult," that Dante
went on and on about
for some 317 pages.

And, I do appreciate
your persistence. It's nice
to have you here, now. Though,
the things I place my sense of you in
are no longer things of the future,
nor that the things of the past
will come back to roost.

That girl from Belgrade
was never going to love me.

And I'm grateful each morning
I get up and write, that I did not
receive tenure at some university.

No… you belong solely to dreams
of my daughter's eventual healing.

And that I might, somehow,
continue to be worthy of
my wife and her love.

LOVE

Here in the fifth act
of the grand human opera,
I hope you have the last word.

You, the only version of God
that I still sometimes consider.

I'm not sure what else to say.
My pen is rolling its eyes
at this attempt to write
you an ode—while all
the poets who made it in
to heaven hold their sides
in a sick, heaving laughter.

But those bards and drunks
should remember: you are
the only one who would've
let them through the gates.

It's just that I wrote an ode
for faith, and one for hope,
and I don't like even numbers.

Something similar to the way
the heart-shape we attribute
to you has no straight lines.

The poets and prophets—
from Moses to Hafiz...
Shakespeare to The Beatles—

tell us that you are it, all there is,
all we need. And I can't think
of anyone more deserving
of that great praise.

THE SINGER

~ for Jimmy LaFave, May 14, 2017

His life, cut short, maybe
by jealous Muses, carried
more soul in a G chord,
followed by a C, then D,
than a century of churches
singing hymns in lock-step
with an unyielding organist.

We heard as much sorrow
and honesty in the spaces
between words and lines,
and we saw so much more,
and farther, when he'd sing
and strum with his eyes shut.

His voice was like a bonfire
that popped and cracked…
and roared in the blue night.

How long can a thing like that
burn, before the trees are gone,

and all the songs finally sung?

    But… a tune like his
        will never die…

even when the earth
is all used up and decides
to dim the lights on the stage,

        something… someone…
        somewhere out there…

will hear his lonesome echo
and start humming along.

Author Bio

Nathan Brown is an author, songwriter, and award-winning poet currently living in Wimberley, Texas.

He holds a PhD in English and Journalism from the University of Oklahoma and served as Poet Laureate for the State of Oklahoma in 2013 and 2014.

Nathan has published roughly seventeen books. Among them is *Don't Try*, a collection of poems co-written with songwriter and Austin Music Hall-of-Famer, Jon Dee Graham. His *Oklahoma Poems* anthology was a finalist for the Oklahoma Book Award. *Karma Crisis: New and Selected Poems* was a finalist for the Paterson Poetry Prize. His earlier book, *Two Tables Over*, won the 2009 Oklahoma Book Award. He's also recorded several CDs of original music.

For more, go to: **brownlines.com**

ALSO BY NATHAN BROWN

Anthologies

Oklahoma Poems, and Their Poets
Agave: A Celebration of Tequila

CDs

Driftin' Away
The Why in the Road
Gypsy Moon
The Streets of San Miguel

MEZCALITA
PRESS

An independent publishing company
dedicated to printing and promoting the
poetry, fiction, and non-fiction of musicians
who want to add to the power and reach of
their important voices.